Zoé de.Las Cases

SECRET TOKYO

Color Your Way to Calm

Little, Brown and Company

New York   Boston   London

Little, Brown and Company
Hachette Book Group
1290 Avenue of the Americas, New York, NY 10104
littlebrown.com

First North American Edition: October 2015
Originally published as *Japon Secret* in France by Éditions Marabout, October 2014

Little, Brown and Company is a division of Hachette Book Group, Inc.
The Little, Brown name and logo are trademarks of Hachette Book Group, Inc.

The publisher is not responsible for websites (or their content) that are not owned by the publisher.

The Hachette Speakers Bureau provides a wide range of authors for speaking events. To find out more, go to hachettespeakersbureau.com or call (866) 376-6591.

ISBN 978-0-316-26584-3
Library of Congress Control Number: 2015944907

10 9 8 7 6 5 4 3 2 1

WW

Printed in the United States of America

Zoé de Las Cases is the artistic director of a creative agency in Paris.

THIS BOOK BELONGS TO:

....

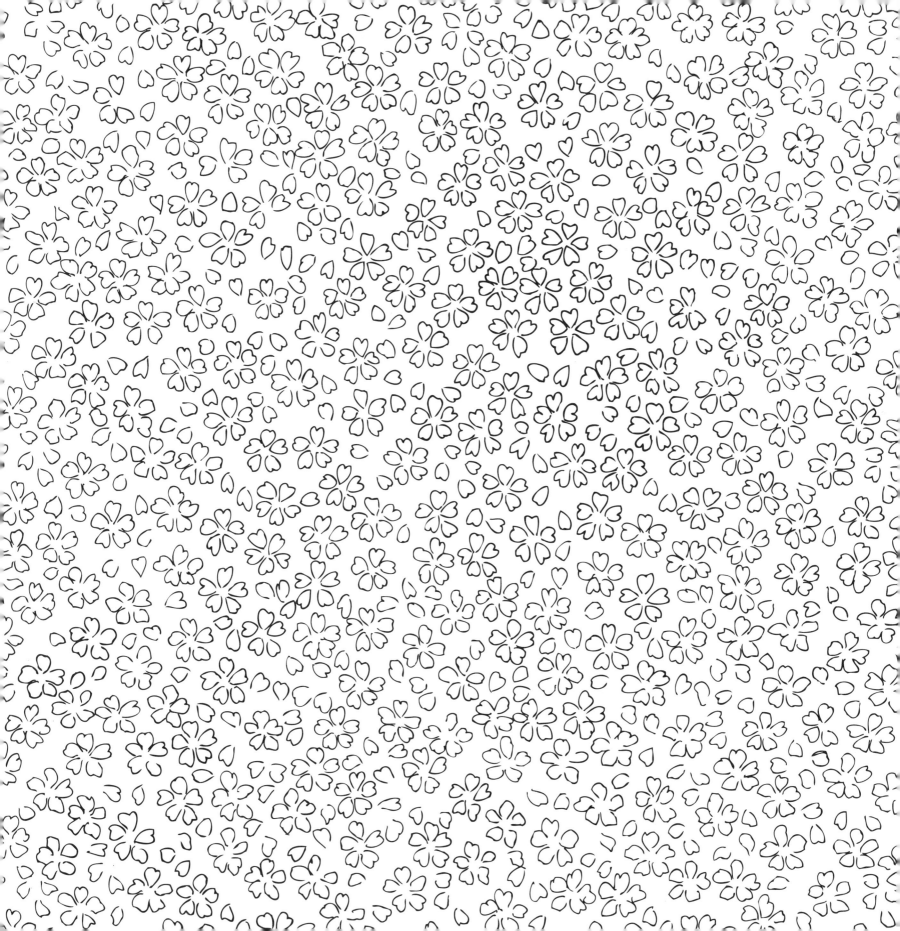

WELCOME TO
MY SECRET JAPAN!

Japan's elegance, refinement, and sophistication make it the ideal destination. Let the beauty and harmony of this land cast its enchanting spell on you.

Stroll past the shop windows of Tokyo and lose yourself in the hustle and bustle of this futuristic and exciting city dotted with incredible temples and museums.

Travel to Kyoto, where the spectacle of this ancient city lit up with lanterns is a seductive and wonderful sight. Everything is a visual delight, from the delicious and refined cuisine to the *ryokans:* historic inns displaying traditional Japanese architecture.

Come with me to the distant land of Japan and immerse yourself in its vibrant culture and natural beauty. Your pens and pencils will capture the colors of this magical and ancient country.

Take your time, relax, and give your imagination free rein as you bring the Land of the Rising Sun to vivid life.

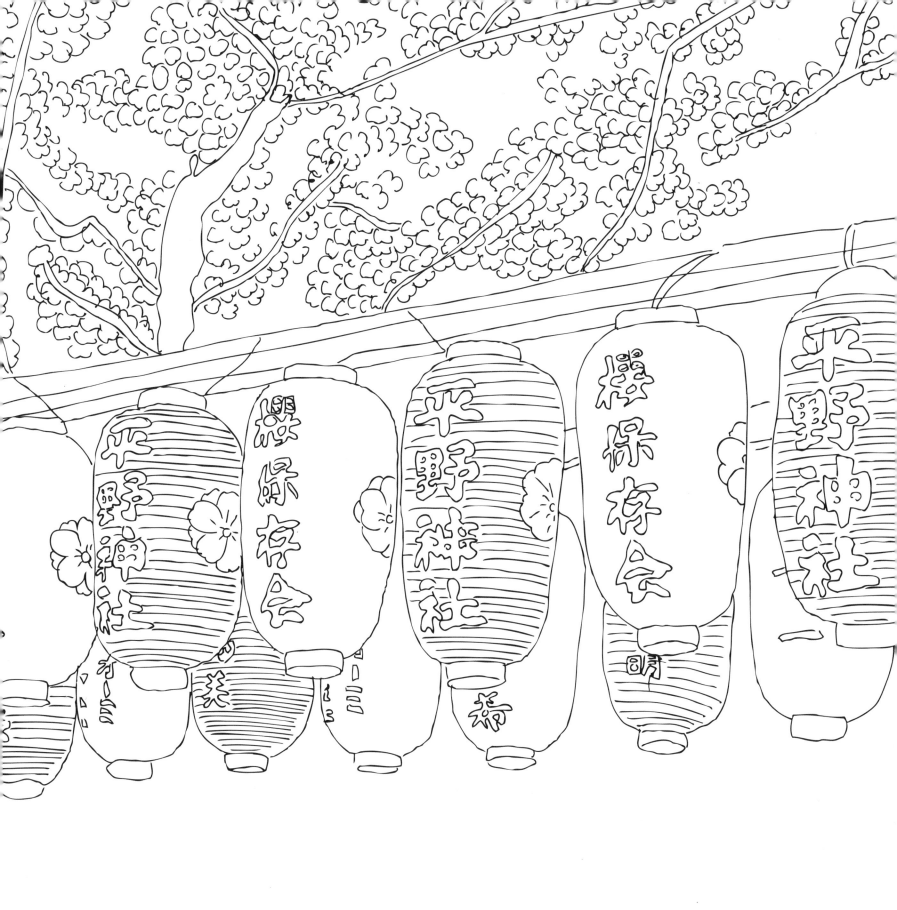

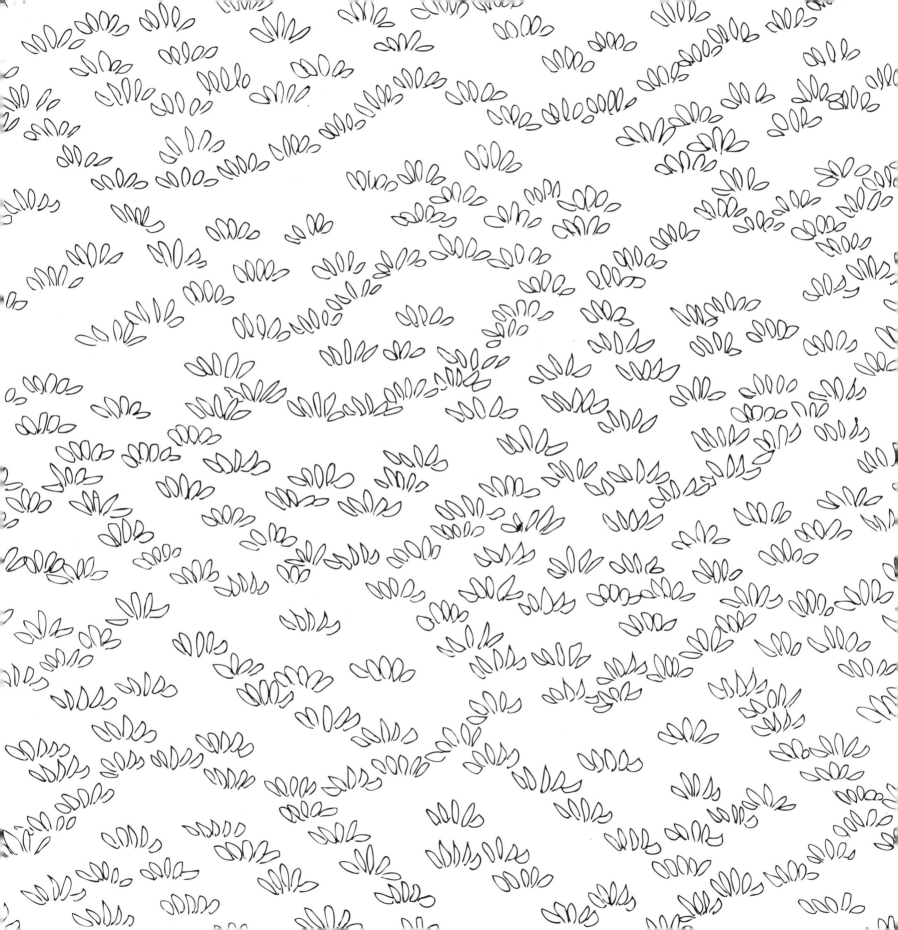

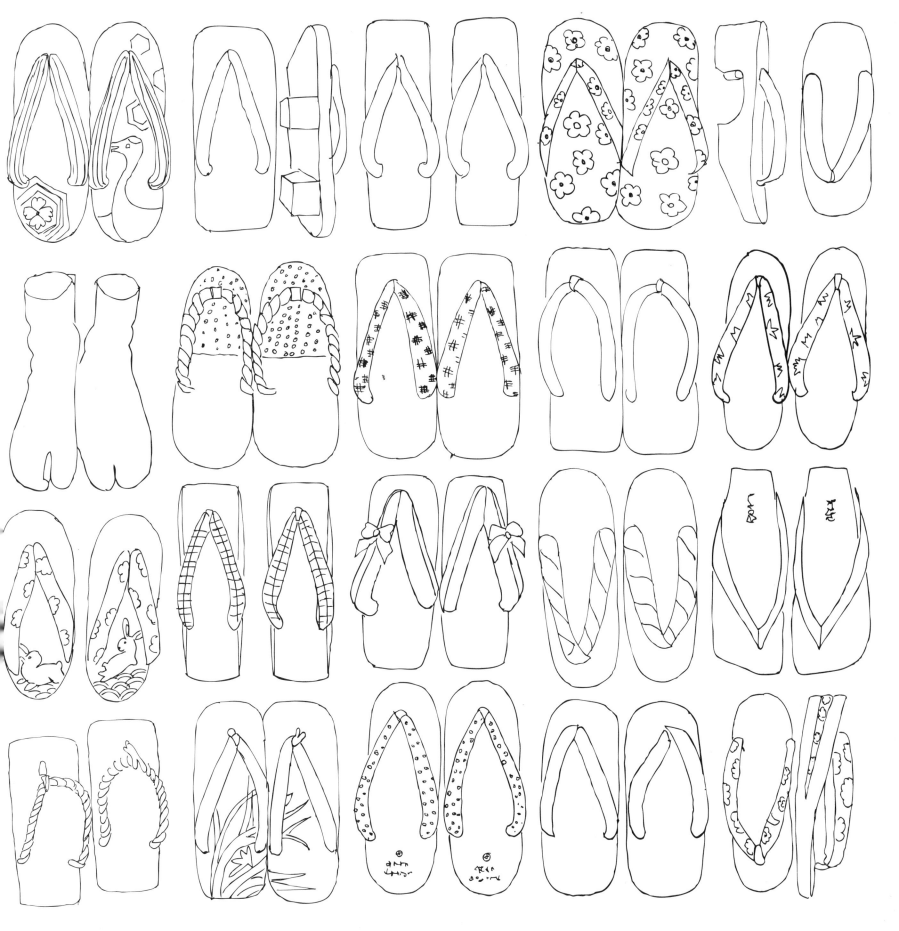

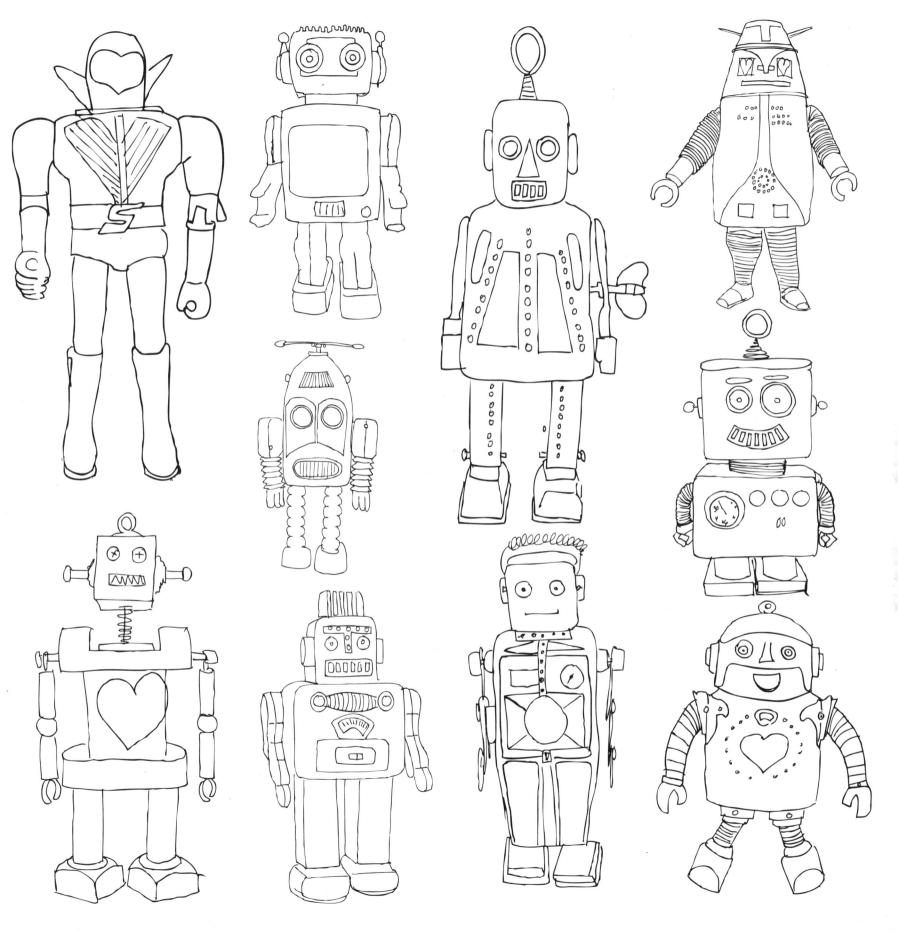

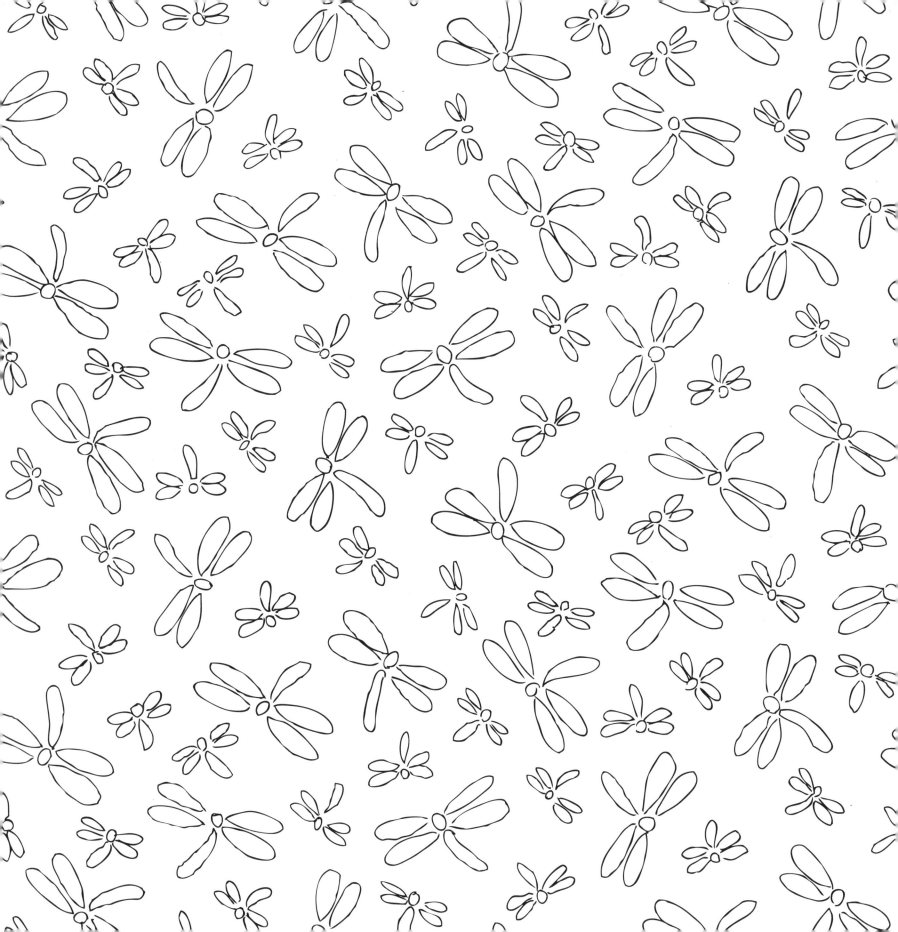

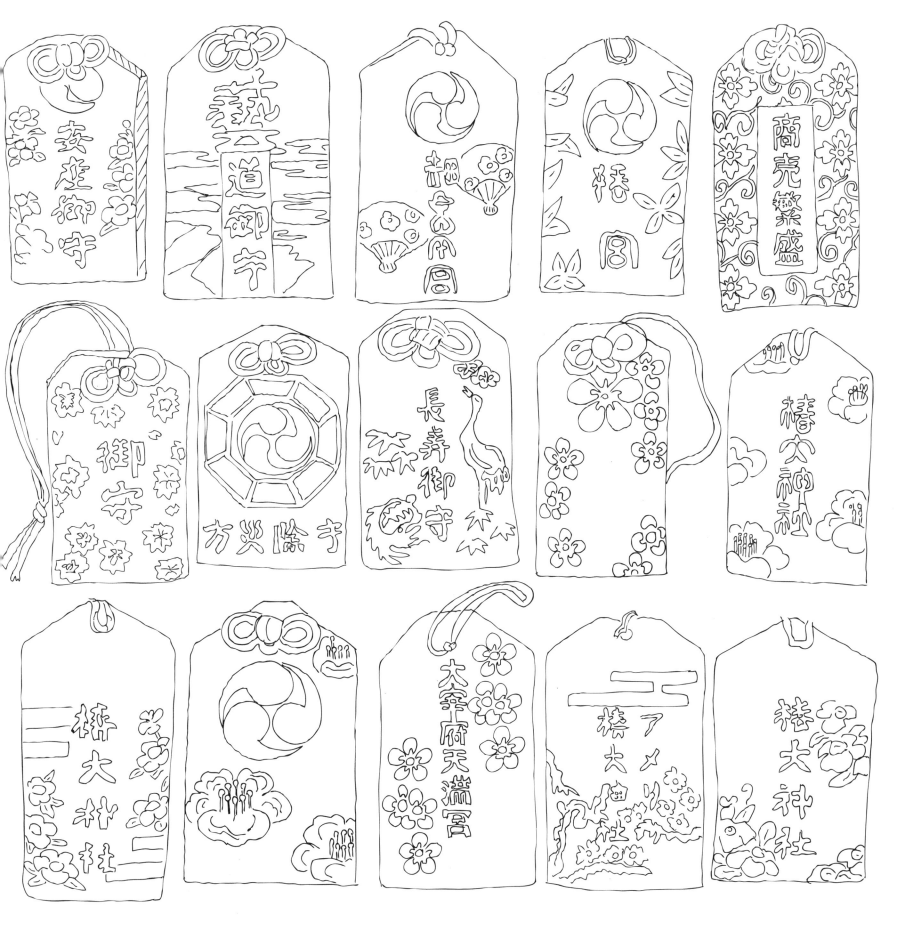

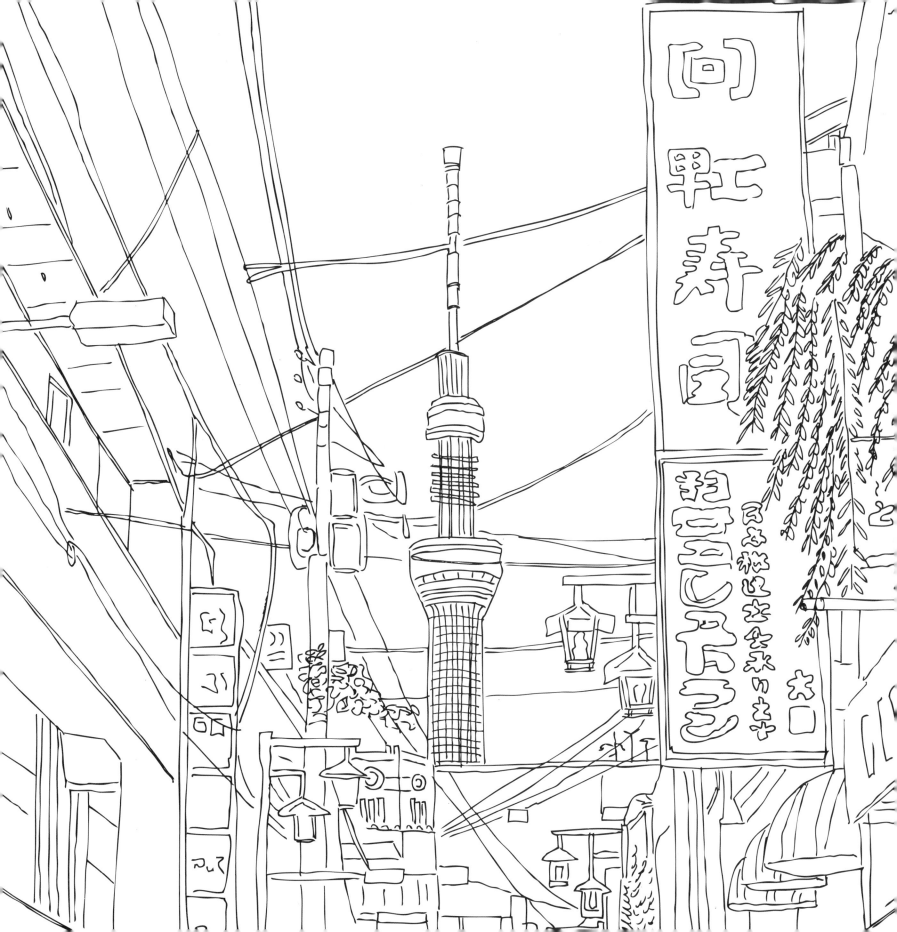

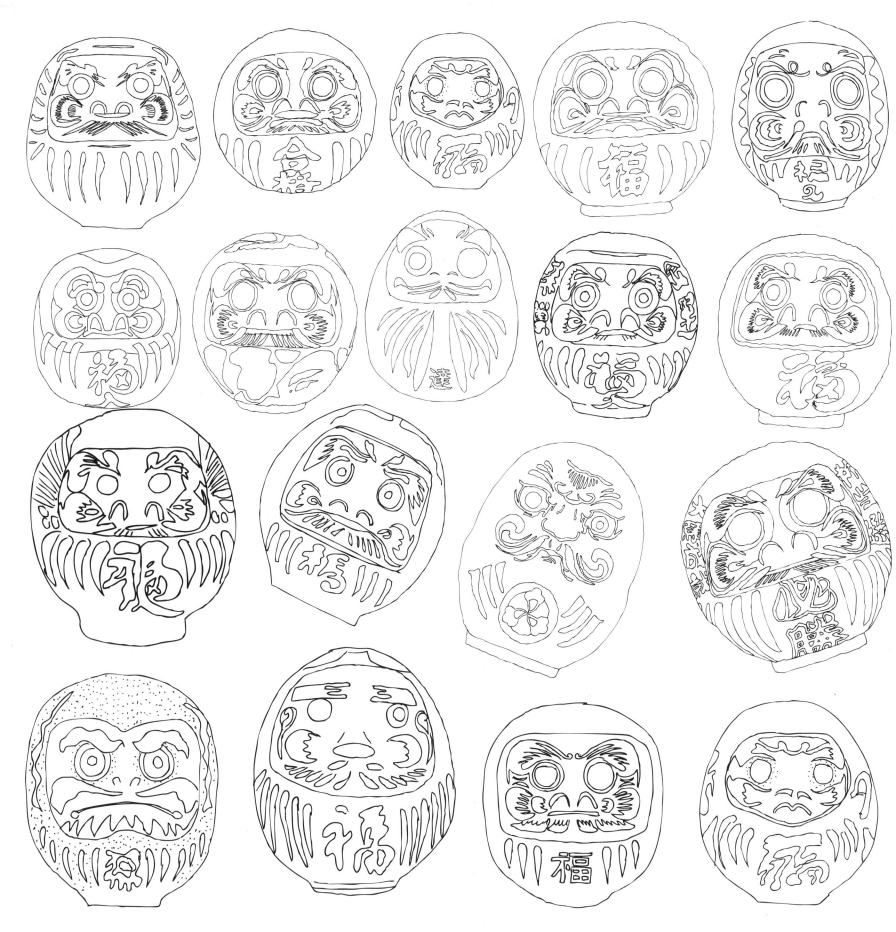

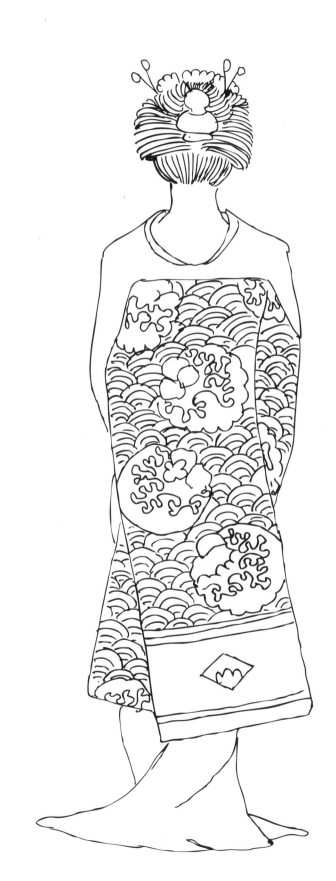

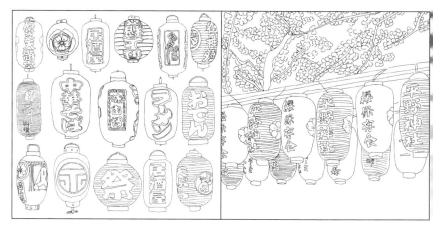

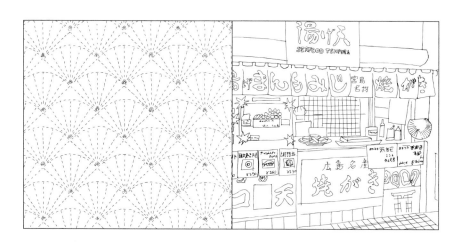

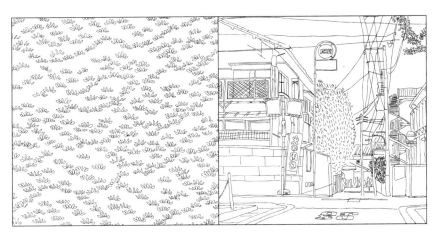

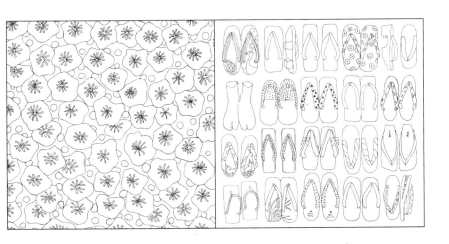

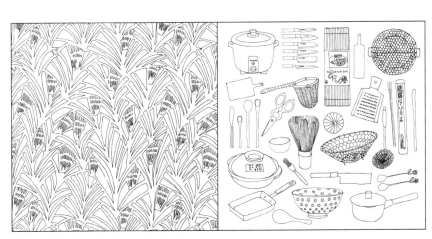

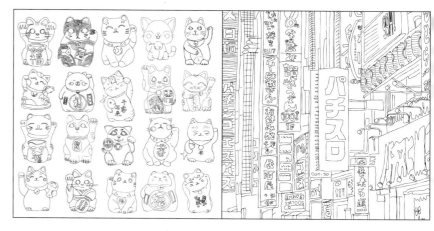

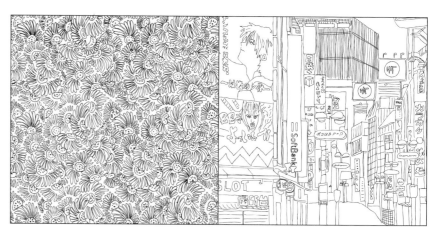

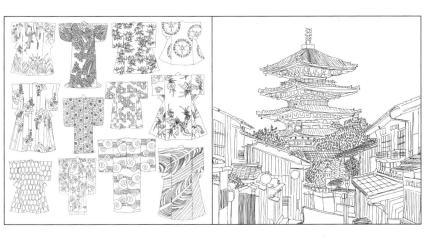

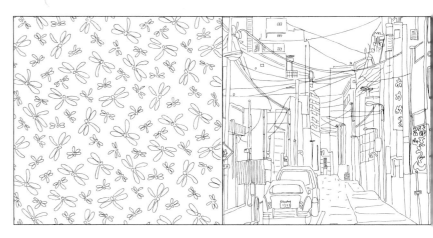
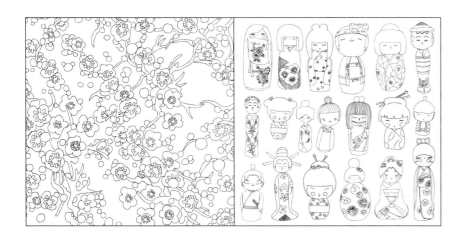
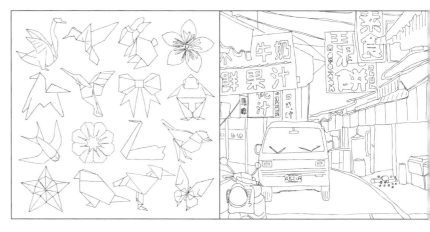

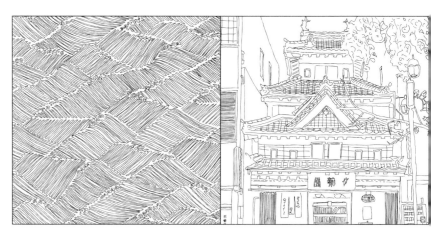

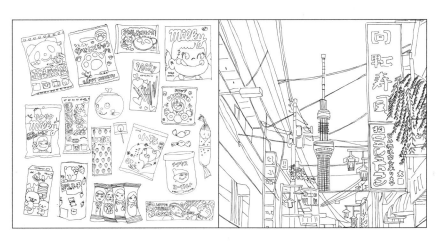

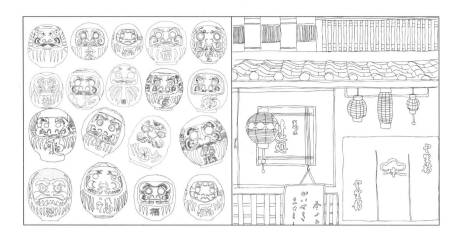

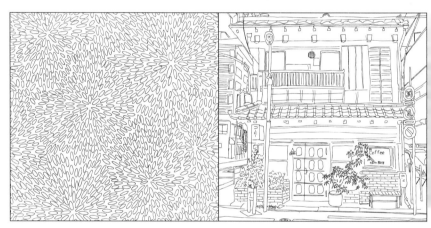

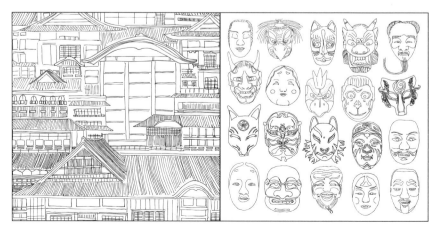